Born in the year
Geboren im Jahr

1973

Astrological character profiles
for every day of the year

Astrologische Charakterprofile
für jeden Tag des Jahres

Bibliografische Information der Deutschen Nationalbibliothek:
Die Deutsche Nationalbibliothek verzeichnet diese Publikation
in der Deutschen Nationalbibliografie; detaillierte bibliografische
Daten sind im Internet über http://dnb.dnb.de abrufbar.

© 2017 Christoph Däppen

christoph.daeppen@bluewin.ch

Herstellung und Verlag:
BoD – Books on Demand, Norderstedt

ISBN 9783746034737

The present paper contains diagrams of the astrological determined character profiles for every day of the year 1973. The data points in the diagrams are depicting the manifestations regarding the following character traits in the scheme of the so-called „Big Five" of psychology:

N: Neuroticism
E: Extraversion
O: Openness (to Experience)
A: Agreeableness
C: Conscientiousness

The underlying astrological model and the applied methods of calculation used for these diagrams are described in a separate work. (→ §)

The diagrams have two scales: one is „absolute" (left) and one is „relative" (right). The data points connected with the solid line relate to the absolute scale; those connected with the dotted line relate to the relative, i.e. percent scale. The relative value thus shows the percentage of the corresponding absolute value compared to the sum of all absolute values deviating from the average or zero line. Values above the average line express higher manifestations of the corresponding character trait and vice versa. The lines connecting the dots have no special meaning except for the purpose of helping to visualize the data points and their spatial distribution within the diagram. The calculation method for determing the absolute values (based on the Swiss Ephemeris tables) is described in the work mentioned above.

The diagrams exhibited as follows do not imply any propositions beyond the findings and considerations that have been made in the work mentioned above, especially regarding the possibility of gender related differences. Readers are invited to critically examine and openly discuss the revealed diagrams in terms of significance, accuracy and further possible use.

Das vorliegende Werk enthält die Diagramme der astrologischen Charakterprofile für jeden Tag des Jahres 1973. Die Datenpunkte in den Diagrammen zeigen die Ausprägungen hinsichtlich folgender Charaktereigenschaften im Schema der sogenannten „Big Five" der Psychologie:

N:	Neuroticism	- Neurotizismus
E:	Extraversion	- Extraversion
O:	Openness (to Experience)	- Offenheit (für Erfahrungen)
A:	Agreeableness	- Verträglichkeit
C:	Conscientiousness	- Rigidität

Das den Diagrammen zugrunde liegende astrologische Modell und die applizierten Berechnungsmethoden sind in einer separaten Studie beschrieben. (→ § ; siehe dort auch die deutschen Fachbegriffe)

Die Diagramme haben zwei Skalen: eine „absolute" (links) und eine „relative" (rechts). Die mit der ausgezogenen Linie verbundenen Datenpunkte beziehen sich auf die absolute Skala; jene mit der gestrichelten Linie verbundenen beziehen sich auf die relative, d.h. prozentuale Skala. Der relative Wert drückt somit aus, welcher prozentuale Anteil der entsprechende absolute Wert an der Summe aller absoluten Wertabweichungen von der Null- bzw. Mittellinie hat. Werte über der Mittellinie indizieren höhere Ausprägungen des betreffenden Charaktermerkmals und Werte darunter entsprechend tiefere. Die die Punkte verbindenden Linien haben selber keine spezielle Bedeutung, sie dienen lediglich der Visualisierung der Datenpunkte bezüglich ihrer räumlichen Verteilung im Diagramm. Die Methode zur Berechnung der absoluten Werte (basierend auf den Swiss Ephemeris Tabellen) ist in der erwähnten Studie beschrieben.

Die im folgenden vorgelegten Diagramme implizieren keine Aussagen, die über die in der oben genannten Studie präsentierten Befunde und Erwägungen hinaus gehen, insbesondere die Möglichkeit von geschlechtsbedingten Unterschieden betreffend. Die Leser sind eingeladen, die gezeigten Diagramme hinsichtlich Aussagekraft,

Treffsicherheit und weiterer Verwendungsmöglichkeit kritisch zu prüfen und offen zu diskutieren.

§ Christoph Däppen: Die Planeten der Präsidenten – Einblicke in eine neue Astrologie; BoD 2015. ISBN 978-3-7386-0655-3.

19.01.1973

20.01.1973

21.01.1973

25.01.1973

26.01.1973

27.01.1973

28.01.1973

29.01.1973

30.01.1973

28.04.1973

29.04.1973

30.04.1973

31.05.1973

01.06.1973

02.06.1973

03.06.1973

04.06.1973

05.06.1973

09.07.1973

10.07.1973

11.07.1973

23.08.1973

24.08.1973

25.08.1973

24.11.1973

25.11.1973

26.11.1973

27.11.1973

28.11.1973

29.11.1973

30.11.1973

01.12.1973

02.12.1973

15.12.1973

16.12.1973

17.12.1973

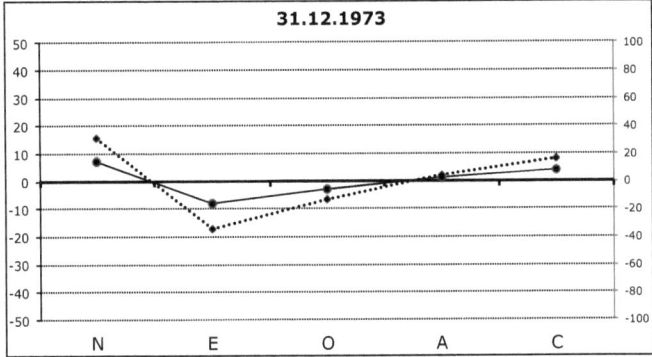